GRAY DAWN

DR. CAROL SING

AuthorHouse™
1663 Liberty Drive
Bloomington, IN 47403
www.authorhouse.com
Phone: 1 (800) 839-8640

Published by AuthorHouse 01/19/2018

ISBN: 978-1-5462-2539-3 (sc)
978-1-5462-2540-9 (e)

Print information available on the last page.

This book is printed on acid-free paper.

This book is dedicated to the love of my life, my husband, Gary Sing, and to the unmitigated support of our beloved son, Justin.

Acknowledgements

Many thanks to all the participants who shared their lives with me during this period of time. I will be forever grateful for their kindness, concern, help, and trust. Linda Blumenthal, my editor, spent hours dissecting, correcting, and suggesting changes. Her insight and due diligence made this publication possible in its present form. John Banks Jr has been brilliant in ensuring the artwork you see displayed was integrated professionally into the final product. Thank you to all the artists that donated their work on the Internet, so that people could enjoy each piece without charge. The artwork was exceptional and added a great deal to the book. Deepest love is sent to my family, which never wavered, through all the experiences encountered and worked through. Life would never be the same without their support. Finally, thanks to Authorhouse for giving the effort a voice. They have been right there for me all the way.

-Carol Sing

Foreword

I want to take you on a journey that may alter your "mindscape." This is a book of mental snapshots taken while people were caught in a situation not of their own choosing. Poetry provides us an avenue to share the thoughts of others in the hope of increasing understanding for what we experienced in the world of the incarcerated, along with those "outside" helping, and the suffering they endured. The emphasis is on various adaptations made to ensure mental and physical survival…sometimes heroic, and about the good people that helped us along the way. Yes, these poems were written in a prison camp during the years 2015-2017 and then in a halfway house, during 2017.

Here are poems of passion. I, and the people and events that made these poems possible, are reaching out to you through the beauty of language.
Carol Sing #19664-081
9-6-17

Table of Contents

Excerpt of Sentencing Decision as Background Information:

This was an amazing case, executed completely outside the normal protections of an established court system. Using the ubiquitous conspiracy theory, which allows sentencing for intent, you will see how *a U.S. citizen can be sentenced to a lengthy term just for presumably thinking about something. (Read the story in my next book, due out in 2018, entitled, No Burden of Proof.)*

In the 10th Circuit Court appeal decision, here is the essence of what was declared: "The District Court had ample evidence, too, to infer that Ms. Sing knew about the information contained in Mr. Timmerman's files [the Defendant, a Utah attorney-in-fact]. Ms. Sing would serve as the resident agent [filing Nevada corporations and corporations sole] for those soles created by Mr. Timmerman, while Mr. Timmerman would refer clients to Ms. Sing to file corporations in Nevada. It could reasonably be inferred that the defendants intended, had their scheme succeeded, to shield their clients from collection of the amounts they owed the IRS at the time they engaged the defendants' services."[1]

You will note an assumption here of intent that never existed. Mr. Timmerman found our registered agent services on the Internet. They were always HIS clients. The duties of a resident/registered agent are to file and renew Nevada corporations. Without exception, Mr. Timmerman's clients testified to that fact at trial and pretrial, as documented in court transcripts. The taxes in question were drawn from a spreadsheet, *not admitted at trial by court order*, which was apparently prepared by the IRS for the trial, dating from 1988-2002. This was up to 16 years *before* I met the first set of Mr. Timmerman's clients, on April 23, 2004.

---

[1] Pages 4-5, Appellate Case: 15-4022 Document: 01019648434 Date Filed: 06/29/2016 10th Circuit Court Appeal Decision

Even by then, most of the collection concerns had been resolved, as there is a 10-year statute of limitation for collection of taxes. Going back to my knowledge of the files, I have never been to Mr. Timmerman's home office in Utah and have never seen his files, as alleged! (In the upcoming book, you will see the word "inference" many times, but never PROOF.) Throughout history, you may have noted many examples of persecution for presumed thinking about a defined, politically unpopular subject. In this case, it is the IRS's perception of the Corporation Sole. You may be amazed where that same line of thought can take you in our country today.

No Greater Love—Vignette

Feeling overwhelms words, but I will try to describe my husband, the focus of the first poem. Heartbroken, yet hopeful, he lives through our continuing separation of space and time. His loyalty is unfailing, and sometimes his heart is at the bursting point. Beginning as a talented sportsman, he once said to me that he never wanted to hurt people in the many games he played. Segue to the present, 45 years later, he works with special children in the public school system. His chain of kind acts remains unbroken.

No Greater Love

Beyond the breaking waves, a lone man rides in his canoe.

Scanning the horizon,

He searches endlessly for a figure,

So close to his heart, so dear to him.

The salt spray caresses his brow,

And he feels at one with the sea.

So kind, so good, so loyal, this man.

Why must he wait?

Because "they" have taken her away.

Suddenly, his senses reel towards

An ethereal energy, not yet formed.

Concern creases his brow as he watches and waits.

Slowly, he becomes conscious of a sound,

So soft, so enticing.

Whispers skim along the waves, only for him.

His conch shell poised, he captures these sounds.

"I must understand," he cries out.

Carefully, he puts the shell to his ear.

"She will return," it echoes. "She will return."

Birthday Soliloquy and Where is My Son?—Vignette

What do you consider the most important characteristics to look for in ours and others' children? To me, love for our fellow man, respect, loyalty, perseverance, honesty, and coping skills. If these are highly valued, parents will teach them. These are what we endeavored to instill in our children. Upon reaching maturity, our son, Justin, did display all of these characteristics and more. We could not ask for a more wonderful son on whom we shower love every day of our lives. This man gave his love, money, time, energy, and endless patience while helping to get his mom through a seemingly endless experience. Kudos to him and to all the other children out there who wait for their moms' return. (Our only other child, Dawn, died in 2000 of pancreatic cancer. The book cover is designed to portray her presence. The blue sky reflects a sea, where her ashes are scattered. In the upper left sector, gray clouds represent her demise. On the middle right, the ray of sun breaking across the horizon tells us of hope and endurance, for the clouds have been pierced.)..a new dawn, a new beginning.)

A Birthday Soliloquy

What is a son?

Bonded forever.

Cut from the same genetic material,

This marvel of manhood

Stands tall among peers.

How do you define someone,

A cut above?

Here's the heart and soul of it:

An intelligent man,

A kind and honest man,

Generous and well-mannered,

Beyond expectations.

This man, our son,

Rises above the foray

To soar with the eagles

On each new day,

Taking the choice to make a difference

So things can be better.

To heed the call, and be free,

To forgive and move on.

Now is his time,

To celebrate life,

Live to the fullest.

This man is a leader,

Actualizing impossible dreams,

On the horizon of eternal space.

Where is My Son?

In the orchid by the door.

Look closely at its center.

See, there, a tiny, smiling face

Appears in greeting.

Look up at the clouds.

You see, he is smiling down at me,

His expression changing in rhythm

With atmospheric measures.

Ah, now he appears in the sun's rays,

So ephemeral, so wistful.

And, there, see in the wings of the hawk,

A gentle, unchanging face of pure peace.

What? Is that my reflection in the water?

No, it is my son, as geese ruffle the pond's surface,

Sending sensations of love.

And, here at the window,

The reflection of him

Streams through the light.

And you thought he was away.

No, he never was. Look around you; he is here, as pure love.

The Light--Vignette

Our daughter-in-law is a gem. Unpretentious, she goes along her way quietly, changing lives. She helps when reaching out seems hopeless. Yet, changes occur…subtle changes that might go unnoticed, except for the subliminal awareness that things are now somewhat better. The best heroines are unsung. Fly on, oh, precious one.

The Light

The light,

An aura. A glow

Surrounds her beauty

In translucent haze.

Light glints off her flowing hair

Like fireflies in an endless dance.

So pristine, so true

This figure of power.

She reaches towards me

With an awesome force.

I know I will be free,

As she is beckoning me to reunite.

Soft vibrations of pure energy

Transcend the place where she stands.

"Come," she says. "I will take you away

To a better place

Where we can choose to be."

Mindful of our presence

In the endless space of liberation—

"No time, no power, no treachery

Can hold you here," she murmurs.

She stretches to connect, and I grasp her hand.

It is done.

Our Planet—Vignette

Our loyal and unwavering friend visited me every weekend, when my family could not be there to visit me at Camp. She lives over 90 miles away, round-trip; our son lives on the East Coast; my husband is so very far away in southern Nevada. Our friend works with us on environmental causes; hence, the poem about our planet. Hard-working, dedicated and wise, she explicitly defines the meaning of friendship. While I will forever remember those brief hours each weekend of communing with my friend, it is the realization of sacrifice for a cause—planetary healing—on which we communed each weekend, that overrides all.

Our Planet

Blue and green or brown and gray?

Bountiful earth or wasteland?

We are at the crossroads.

What man has done, must be undone

For our very survival depends on it.

Visualize the earth, as evolved,

Green and blue abound.

Ecological balance satisfies the eye

In the precepts of time.

All is well.

Wait.

Money flutters endlessly on the scene.

Production demands;

Encroaching pollution results.

Does greed permeate

Our consciousness?

Does money set us free

Or chain us to an endless trek of blame?

Denial? Injustice?

Stop!

We are alive and free to choose.

Choose life.

Freedom--Vignette

A bundle of talent in this dynamic, intelligent ball of energy. Very fitness conscious, she moves with a muscular, rhythmic grace. Always willing to volunteer, was in every event, either singing or dancing her heart out. What a pleasure to be around her! Wherever she goes, a ray of sunshine goes with her and lights up our lives just by her presence.

Freedom

Surrounded by barbed wire and endless fences,

She walks, oblivious to her surroundings.

A perpetual smile adorns her radiant face,

An inner glow emanating from her being.

Ah, this is a strong force, a pure force

Of joy, peace, happiness, and love.

Her talents unrepressed,

She sees beyond the translucent walls,

For "they" cannot hold her spirit within.

There, you see, she becomes one with the hawk

Circling overhead.

"How free we are!" she cries.

The hawk dips his wings in response.

"So, as the wind allows you to soar,

So, it allows me, for I am connected to you.

I can fly forever because of you.

We are truly free--

As we were meant to be."

A Warden's Humanism…One Heart, The Message and Icon--Vignette

This depicts the only warden I ever met. He was unusually complex, a multi-faceted, multi-layered person. Always willing to help, he listened and arranged solutions. The duties required were many, varied, and challenging, and yet, he made you feel that you could talk to him. Subtlety was his by-word. He did what he could to the best of his ability—a fine and kind man. These poems were written in his honor.

One Heart

Unification of humanity

Or

Division by privilege?

Illusion of caring

Is not caring.

What makes us human?

Following man-made rules

Or

Acting in consort

For the benefit of all?

Where do universal truths lie?

Inside all of us.

The precepts formulated

Are to be carried through.

Cause and effect—

Both must be evaluated before action can occur.

Creativity is destroyed by conformity.

What will you do

To advance a cause?

Or

Has it already been done?

Will you start anew?

Our maxims of freedom, respect, and justice

Represent the ground floor of humanity.

The antithesis wallows in destruction for all.

Choose well.

The stakes are high.

The Message

Murmurs waft through the elephant grass.

The claws of injustice sink deep.

Can he sense the hue and cry?

Where is our leader?

What stays him?

Mindful of the stereotypical fog,

The elite searches.

So grounded are we.

So damaged are they.

A mindset long forsaken

Lingers in the dust.

Each new day starts the histrionics again.

The forebearer of the vanquished

Bravely carries justice in his heart.

He is coming to free us

With the stroke of a pen.

Come, Vanguard, come.

The time is now.

The hour is pressing.

Icon

A dapper figure overlooks the sea of blue,

Reaching out to help the distressed.

Inordinate amounts of responsibility

Swirl in the dazzling currents of change.

Can he bring spontaneous leadership

Amongst the discordant thrust of two worlds colliding?

To push, cajole, punish, restrict, penalize, control,

Juxtaposed with the rehabilitative, nurturing milieu

Sweeping through to reduce the revolving door complex…

Ah, the pinnacles of grace and dignity within this man,

Who finds himself at the crux of change.

Listen to the ancestral call to reason,

Proactively vested for the betterment of all.

Rights sit well on his shoulders and

He becomes the standard bearer of change.

He is willing to stand, to think, to be

A timeless vanguard

Over the entrenched divide.

Chrysalis—Vignette

Here in the epicenter of freedom, this director strives mightily to make a difference. His efforts mark true because of symbiosis. Throughout history, caring has motivated those cared for. He helps build the bridge for people to cross back to life. How important the completion of this cycle is, to break the chains of bondage. Institutionalization can stultify most human ambition, given sufficient time. The director must be an emancipator with great wisdom. Surpassing our own expectations is a worthy challenge he willingly accepts.

Chrysalis

In a swirling storm of dust

A nearly invisible man

Makes his presence known.

Quietly, with prescience,

He begins to speak:

"Mass incarceration.

The bane of America."

Winds carry his words,

In an endless array of sounds.

Entrenched corruption

Cannot dissuade his mission,

To heal, to make whole once again.

They are all important to him,

These socially distorted prisoners,

Suffering from perturbation

Due to loss of freedom.

Reuniting the broken pieces of their lives,

The chaos begins to settle.

He has laid a clear path,

Through his strength of purpose.

An icon of calm,

The dust settles around him.

Now the healed see.

They can follow his way

As he has stilled the storm,

With only his desire to guide.

He succeeds,

In counter-distinction

To the failed perpetrators.

A ray of sunlight emerges,

Permanently scarring their haughty demeanor.

Core Philosophy—Vignette

Caring is at the heart of this kind and concerned woman. She wants success for all she meets, no matter how protracted the history of each individual. With a strong work ethic, she greets each day with an indefatigable drive to do her job well. She is an asset to the half-way house, and one they can ill afford to be without.

Core Philosophy

Adversity and woe

Have demarcated the path

She has traversed.

Her human spirit has risen above

The travails that surround her.

With sparkling eyes

And the fairest of smiles,

She radiates strength and pride.

Though cause screams out experiences,

Her heart never falters.

Ever wise to the environment

Of contentious fugue,

Her reaction survives the moment,

And exemplifies what must be done.

How often has respect and honesty

Played directly on the keys to her soul?

They're there, always,

Like granite in the sea,

A strength for those seeking survival.

A Leader Evolved—Vignette

This amazing woman of grace and charm, is an inspiration to all that come into contact with her. Marked by resiliency, success will always be within her grasp. Her concern for our fellow humans takes her beyond the threshold of normal social interchange. Her courage, without sacrificing basic values, allows her to surpass the usual pathways identified with the attainment of success. Onward, my friend—one person CAN change the world!

A Leader Evolved

This Afghani princess,

Of incomparable beauty,

Tumbles into the world of war.

Striving to help the Americans,

She confronts corruption head on.

She sees,

She hears,

She reports,

And is stung like a bee,

Even to the point of torture.

Extradition.

Betrayal.

Prison.

A never-ending

Devolution into the abyss.

At the bottom, light filters only from above.

Stronger with each upward step—

Her world transforms as it was before.

"In saving my own life, I can save the lives of others."

Wiser now, parameters defined,

She knows how to prevail.

Profundity is the mark.

The Pirates of Penance—Vignette

The complexity of this poem's imagery mirrors the complexity of our relationship. In our separate ways, we were the harbingers of change. We both turned to the resident ground owls—endangered, yet brave, for the real lessons to be learned. These owls clung to life and the concept of freedom, as we did, but they lived by a prison we were forced to inhabit. From them, we learned how to soar in our minds. This lesson spurred us homeward, even though the path was fraught with obstacles. As the owls soared, so did we, eventually to our homes…

The Pirates of Penance

The whirling, invisible walls waft and wane

In the aura of the whispering owl.

Transfixed in the mist, two beings

Of like mind and spirit, goad the darkness.

Silent screams well up from the soil.

What must we do to seal this distress?

How can we mend the cause of unending pain?

But look, the winds of change engulf our minds,

Breathless, as the sense of freedom abounds.

Of what IS freedom made? A soaring eagle? A meaningful life?

Caught in an updraft of swirling words

Combined to grasp meanings for progress—

Feet planted, yet reaching towards the stars.

The road ahead, a beacon of light

Gently beckoning. Let us show you the way.

Clear eyes guide our itinerant travelers

To a path well-trodden, marked by understanding.

They see the owl flying, not in its nest.

Words settle into answers to the questions never asked.

They are free to be; they are earth-born, yet rising.

Who left these treasures? Go see, the beings are with us.

Yes, the pirates of penance will always be near. Forever.

Transcendence—Vignette

This woman reached out to me at the beginning of my incarceration. She showed me the camp's wildlife, cooked her dessert creations, talked with me endlessly, and provided the desperately needed stability so lacking in that compound. She was always there, supplying whatever was needed. Her own life story was fraught with deep disappointments, but she never gave in to them, the entire time we were in the same facility. She was a ray of light, with positive reinforcements, whenever my hopes seemed to falter. I will always remember this solidly-placed friend of humanity. She was wise beyond definition. She was a true friend.

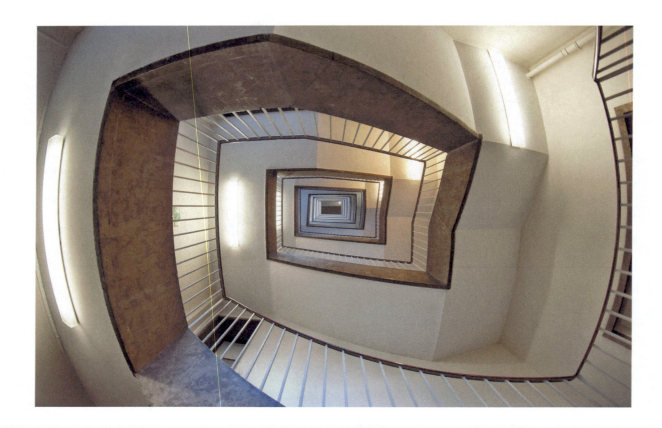

Transcendence

A sunflower rising through the oblique rays of the sun.

Spirit of the mist in shimmering, yet not quite seen, hues.

She embodies the good, the kind, and the empathetic.

Her aura is powerful.

She reaches out.

Will you be willing to grasp her hand

To be anchored, strong and true?

Her future unfolds through a myriad of ideas

With dreams taking shape to live within.

Yes, survival. Yes, rising to a higher plateau

And now soaring to

The firmament for us all

In a parallel world—

Because she wills transcendence.

Starbound—Vignette

When life deals craps, she just smiled and said, "Let's roll again." She was doggedly determined to survive this venue, despite her lengthy sentence. I admire her stamina; she never lost sight of how she would unveil her true self, once free. So many of these stories are twisted from the ubiquitous concept of conspiracy. Guilt by association, tumbling inexorably into someone else's thoughts or dreams, devoid of awareness, all this is at the core.

Reality can be stark, when realizing that an employee is using your property to sell drugs, while you are at work. And, so, years are taken from this older woman. She did not succumb to the ever-changing atmosphere of incarceration…she intends to emerge and begin again. What a marvel of what striving to just be yourself, means. We should all hope she, and the many in her same circumstance, harbor the value of "rising above." There is an end point here. She, and thousands of others, will realize it.

It is then that the critical juncture starts, and the inevitable seeds are sewn. May she grow a garden, and gift it to the suppressed, as a symbol of new beginnings.

Starbound

Alone, she walks beside

The quiet stream.

Her dreams reflected

In the dancing waters.

How often she comes here

In her mind.

The rapidly moving clouds

Carry her away,

To a wider expanse of

Perpetual motion.

Finally, she sees it forming,

The meaning of her life.

A purpose, a goal,

Something worth striving for—

Endurance. Perseverance. Determination.

All demarcate the path,

Glinting off the clouds.

It is here.

It is now.

It is real.

It is enough.

"How I have longed for this,"

She whispers to the wind.

A gentle answer.

It is time.

Steadfast—Vignette

This woman preceded me in Camp and followed me to the halfway house. The marvel is her perpetual smile and spirit of hope. She is endlessly inventive as to how to create something out of literally nothing. That includes her revised career in medicine, which encircles, but does not duplicate, her now-prohibited former career. Despite all, there is no bitterness, no cynicism, only the view of a brighter future.

I finally understand the concept, "Patience is a virtue." For those that survive this experience, patience is the only way. If there ever was a perfect fit for an alternative universe, this is it— the survivors of incarceration.

Steadfast

A figure of determination,

Yet gentle.

This woman of courage and kindness

Listens and watches

For opportunities to help herself and others.

Little gets by her steady gaze.

In this confined world

Of crafted miasma,

Only a clever, intent person

Can sift through the fog

To bring forth the answers.

We can all progress

Because of her insight.

A guiding light

Critical in the maelstrom

Of swirling words and sordid actions.

We thank you, Avatar.

Ode to Eagle Feather—Vignette

Proudly she represents Native America. She is pure of heart, with undiminished purpose, to lead her tribe. Although in her early 20s, she carried within her the wisdom of the ages. Admiration of her spirit came easily. (She also wrote a poem to me, of which an excerpt is included in this book.)

On her departure, she gave me her treasured eagle feather, which was by her side throughout her entire journey here. Words fail me in describing that moment of interchange—across cultures and time.

Ode to Eagle Feather

As the dazzling array

Of snowflakes fall to the earth,

Each one different

Each one new,

So Eagle Feather emerges

Metamorphosed with the new dawn.

Unique in every facet,

She rises to the call,

Sees every outstretched arm

As to her own.

Leadership—

From the hawks and eagles,

She draws her spirit.

Chains unlocked, she soars.

Now she sees and

Becomes one with the universe.

She presses higher,

For aloft, life's problems diminish.

Now she knows!

The words of her ancestors

Fall softly on the air.

Lead, Eagle Feather.

"I will lead well," she sighs into the wind.

Air currents carry her

To her new horizon.

"From here, I will launch."

Mentor—a poem written to Carol Sing from Eagle Feather

I could see it in your eyes, and real eyes realize.

I look to you and see the wise.

Gives me hope.

You give the best advice.

Just like the eagle,

I see you soaring above it all.

The knowledge you give to the weak is strength and

In so many ways you made me strong.

By Eagle Feather, age 22

Fortitude—Vignette

A personable woman, of a sweet nature, she is subtle in her approach, after concerted thought. In a halfway house, this personality blossoms for the benefit of the residents. Of importance, the respect generated is mutual, one hallmark of recovery. She reminds me of one residing in Camelot—a surreal setting, yet attainable, in part, for our setting is also an aberration. She may not realize how invaluable her presence is. Now, she can become a small part of history.

Fortitude

Quietly she goes on her way,

Mindful of the responsibility she bears.

A kind and generous spirit,

That dares to deviate from

The invisible lines separating us.

Here is an invaluable cross-identification

Surmounting the usual pretense.

Does it matter?

To her, it does.

At the epicenter is realization

Of the human condition

And the need to return.

Here, normal life becomes abnormal,

Which must be undone.

She can do this.

Isn't it amazing

How the simplest concepts

Of human nature

Flow right past most?

Ennui, indifference, arrogance

Replace empathy.

It takes a genuine glow of warmth

To penetrate the shrouds of darkness.

To lead to a better place,

Is her solitary mission.

Many lives will be enhanced.

Bonding, not veils of intrigue,

Is the harbinger of positive social change.

A humble road traveled,

With monumental results.

Be at peace, Kind One.

You are right.

Saint George—Vignette

It took months to understand this man who reminds me of the TV character, "Lieutenant Colombo." Both men portray such a magical accolade. For those failing to perceive the real substance of Saint George's personality, a great opportunity is lost. His unique persona is a joy to others, but it only manifests upon mutual understanding. The whys of the layering dissolve upon connection, born of respect.

Saint George

Place a crown on a man,

He instantly becomes king.

Penetrate layers of complexity,

And discover a Saint George.

A nuance, a flair,

What you see is not really there.

Honed skills of perception,

Fall hard before deception.

The king?

Symbolism.

The saint?

Remote and nearly impenetrable.

A man portraying the jester,

In all seriousness.

A crowd of whispers

Hint of this powerful being.

Entrenched in a shroud.

His sparkling eyes

Capture the strength within.

Through self-proclaimed humility,

He defines his intent and purpose...

A Linear Dream—Vignette

This had to be the most difficult story for me to write. Based on a single phone call, she got 8 years taken from her life. She became my best friend in the facility. We planned a business, which we were to launch together. Always interested in fitness, we worked out together nearly daily. Her cheery smile and calm disposition were a welcome change to our daily struggles.

Before this camp, she had been in a Federal Correctional Institution, where she had contracted pneumonia. As a result, she needed medication to regulate the flow of fluids to her lungs. This precisely regulated medication also affected how her heart functioned.

Due to a "snafu," the administration of her medication at the camp resulted in a doubling of the dosage. This caused deleterious side effects, resulting in an appointment with her pulmonary specialist, who was to meet her in a regular hospital room.

Although she was admitted to the hospital, she was not met by the pulmonary specialist. She was admitted to the emergency room, assigned to a bed, and died 9 days later—swollen up like a balloon. Her death was reported to us by Camp staff who visited her.

The strangest twist to the story is that her medical orders, which she showed me, stated specifically, "DO NOT ADMIT TO EMERGENCY." She left a daughter and 3 grandchildren, whom she was to reunite with in February of 2017. She died in the summer of 2016.

A Linear Dream

That irrepressible smile.

The undeniable strength behind it.

She was determined to make a change,

To make a real difference.

She was genuine—no fair-weather friend.

Always striving to do better—be better.

So, as her years in prison were coming to an end,

She reached out to share her knowledge and experiences with those needing her help.

Goals, plans, and dreams were all thought out and completed.

Like so many others, she counted the months.

Departure was on the horizon.

She often said, "I may never have left home, if I hadn't come this way."

Now, the prospect running an employment agency

Specializing in finding jobs for those formerly incarcerated

Seemed as exciting as anything she had ever done.

She had a genuine support network now, where before she walked alone.

Because of you, this and all future employment agencies will have a plaque

Dedicated to your memory—an integral part of the décor.

Success will bring trust funds to your grandchildren.

It is through your initial efforts that they will benefit.

Thank you for just being here.

All who knew you were deeply enriched.

Herstory—Vignette

This poem was written for and read at a Black History Month event at the Camp. The whole range of inmates participated, bringing their unique talents to the festivities. Working mostly with our minds, we provided a respite and temporary escape from the normally controlled and structured environment and its 12-cents-an-hour, work-a-day world.

Herstory

What does race mean?

The Human Race.

Where did it originate?

In Africa.

Why do humans cover the earth?

Migration.

But we look different—

On the outside.

Well, why is that?

In part by exposure to the sun.

What?

The more sun exposure, the more pigmentation of the skin.

But, humans have different values and norms.

Different cultures result from varying adaptations to their environment.

Why are some cultures seemingly more advanced than others?

The harsher the environment, and the more varied the population, the more adaptations we see.

So, say in London, there would be more adaptation than in New Guinea.

Yes, if the environment provides what humans need to survive and the humans are isolated,

Adaptation remains relatively constant.

How is what we call progress achieved?

Initially, trial and error; then by education, known as passing information on.

That's why educational opportunities have to be equally available.

Yes, because in more progressive societies, education leads to economic success,

And, economic success leads to economic equality.

Precisely.

So, where do we start?

First, by accepting and loving yourself.

And then?

Goal setting and focusing on their attainment.

What about detractions?

Recognize them and move on.

Key words?

NEVER GIVE UP.

Games

The following are do-it-yourself games to be played when you don't want to--**_or can't_** go shopping. The "population" at the Camp had great fun with these invented/modified games.

"Conundrum"

Directions:
1. Get a wide variety of magazines.
2. Look for the thicker pages, like those with expensive ads.
3. Use a large picture from which to cut each puzzle piece. First, cut out the picture part. Make sure not to use overlapping colors among the picture backgrounds. (Example: use only one with a gray background.)
4. Find as many pictures as needed to have each player reconstruct at least 3 puzzle pictures for each game.
5. Cut each picture into large puzzle pieces that will fit together, when reassembled.
6. Mark an "X" on the back of each so the "right side" shows (unmarked). (Note: For interest, I cut each piece asymmetrically, or in geometric shapes.)
7. Spread the pieces out on a table, separating them so they don't overlap. Make sure you put the X-side facing down, so each piece is right-side up.
8. Have the players line up. Each one picks up a piece with part of an object or person showing.
9. The other players view the piece; and, if necessary, pick up another type of picture, not matching an already selected piece. Repeat with each player.
10. Once everyone has their initial piece, set a time limit of 15 minutes for completion of the game.
11. Each player looks through the spread-out pieces and picks them up to match their original piece.
12. Each person assembles the puzzle and returns to select another new puzzle piece, which is shown to the other players.
13. The process is repeated until one person has assembled three puzzles correctly.
14. Then give a prize to the winner.

Note: The players found the game to be fast and exciting. Remember, puzzle pieces must be spread out, right-side up, and not overlapping. This game was only played by adults. For children, the pictures could be adapted to children's pictures—toys, cartoons, etc.

"Scavenger Hunt"

Directions:

Pick a large area to hide your pre-selected items. Riddles have been written for each item. (Answers for the riddles are on a separate, adjoining page.) The person finding the most items wins the game.

Print and hand out copies of the riddles to each player.

1. As Snow White sleeps, you shall not,
   For you must find what Snow White got.

2. One shoe is your first clue.
   Make sure it matches the original hue. (Tell the players the matching shoe color.)

3. A useless item, or so it may seem,
   Until it gains value, when you must clean.

4. Games of chance? Games of skill?
   Mental gymnastics to test your will.

5. By various names, a slipper, a thong…
   Find a pair for the game, and keep moving along.

6. A second-chance tool; you'll need it most days.
   Just find this one, and correct your ways.

7. In close quarters, this item's a must.
   Fail to use daily, and become social dust.

8. A necessity of life, when you take your first sip.
   Without it, there is strife. Keep it close to your lips.

Answers to Scavenger Hunt:

1. Apple
2. Once found, visibly display the other shoe
3. A rag
4. Playing cards
5. Flip-flops
6. An large eraser
7. Deodorant
8. A bottle of water

"Scavenger Hunt": Second Version

1. "Come now, Snow White,
   Take just one bite."
   She did and fell into a swoon.
   Find what sealed her fate
   And you'll see what she ate.
   Only a prince can break through the gloom.

2. A fat little container
   Makes a fine retainer,
   And in it, you will find candy.
   You must look carefully,
   For to find it, you'll see
   That having good candy is dandy.

3. Poker, Bridge, Canasta and Spades
   Helps most of us enjoy the day.
   Sometimes, play for money;
   Other times, just to make the day sunny,
   But you need this in order to play.

4. Never did we think
    That a utensil was jinxed,
    But in a home
    It just keeps disappearing.
    So, lay yourself low,
    As you search with the flow
    To see the utensil reappearing.

5. It's out of place
    In a small, little space,
    So you can't read it right now.
    Look for the one
    Whose title is spun
    From the stories that make you say, "Wow!"

6. Let's salute some décor
    For dinner parties galore.
    And, what do you surmise is most needed?
    Just think what you get
    When your fingers are wet,
    And you might find something unheeded.

7. "Don't touch anything,"
    Said the new-born gosling
    Who struggled to get out of its shell.
    Just like the new shoots,
    Don't pull up the roots,
    But use this for unwanted cells!

8. All through the week
   We continue to seek
   For treasures the mailman delivers.
   First, the egregious pile
   Of things out of style,
   Before we discover the slivers.

9. A TV show, we've learned
   Gives points hard to earn,
   As we strive to remember the names.
   What game is this now?
   Makes us wise like an owl
   And puts all others to shame.

10. Our drive for a shower
    Makes us smell lie a flower.
    But what if there's only just one?
    Find this, and you'll say,
    "It's been fun to play,
    And I think that this game's full of puns."

Answers to the Second Scavenger Hunt:

1. Apple
2. Small jar of good candy
3. Playing cards
4. Paring knife
5. A short-story mystery book
6. A dinner napkin
7. Gardening gloves
8. An envelope containing a canceled or voided check
9. A sign with the name "Jeopardy" written on it
10. Bar of soap

"Find-the-Face" Puzzle--Rules

Directions:

Per the following Maze and Key:

1. There are 44 faces hidden in the puzzle.

2. Some may be asymmetrical or upside down.

3. Once you find a face, circle it with a pencil.

4. If you make a mistake, erase the circle.

5. The person finding the 44 faces correctly in the shortest amount of time, wins.

Note: Some faces are incomplete. If *only eyes and nose are shown, do not count it as a face*.

Find-the-Face Puzzle

Find-the-Face Puzzle Key

Finale

I throw my word ropes to you. May you not use them in a tug of war, but to seek higher ground, and effect social change. You can contact me at **drcarolsing@gmail.com**.

Follow this author in her next exciting book, **No Burden of Proof**, which takes you on a strange and shocking adventure through our jurisprudence system. With full documentation, you will find what cost tax payers millions of dollars, only to discover…truth is far stranger than fiction.